2019
TO MY FRIEND

From your I love
you more friend!
Sandy T.

Little Book of
FRIENDSHIP

Thanks for always being here for me!

new seasons®

Some people search their
whole lives for a friend like you.

A good friend knows the song in your heart and will sing it with you.

Every day with you is like
the first day of spring.

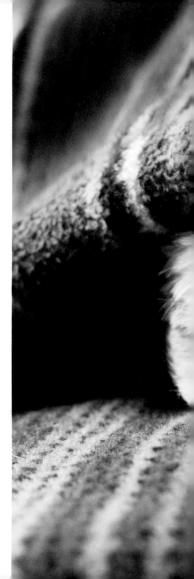

Good friends can talk together; great friends can dream together.

You make my life so
much sweeter.

14

I will never get tired of being your best friend.

Our differences are
what make us stronger.

Together we're unstoppable.

No matter how far apart we are, I'll always feel close to you.

Best friends hold the piece of us that has been missing.

Our friendship keeps me warm,
even on the coldest days.

Friends like you are the
most precious treasure.

Hey buddy,
I got your back.

You've jumped right into my heart!

A good friend is someone
who knows what's on your mind,
even when you haven't said a word.

True friends help us grow.

When I feel down, I know
you'll lift me up.

You'll be my best friend 'til
the cows come home.

When you need to talk,
I'm always here to listen.

I love you to the North Pole and back.

You make my life brighter
and my smile wider.

47

You are one amazing chick.

I will catch you if you fall.

A good friend will push
you to do your best.

I love being close-knit with you.

The day you became my friend, my world became blessed.

You always know what
to say to make me smile.

I know I can count on you to
lead me in the right direction.

Friends like you don't
happen along every day.
I'm glad you happened to me.

Time flies when I'm with you.

You make my heart feel warm and fuzzy.

I'm my best self when I am with you.

You are my strongest support system.

I could spend all day doing
nothing with you.

Thank you for being there for me when I need you the most.

You've left a paw print on my heart.

A best friend will
make sure you never
have to walk alone.

There is no sunset as beautiful as the friendship we share.

You're the best partner in crime.

What a beautiful friendship
we've hatched!

Laughing with you is my favorite thing to do.

Great friends can be found in the most unexpected places.

Know that I'll be by your side,
even when times are tough.

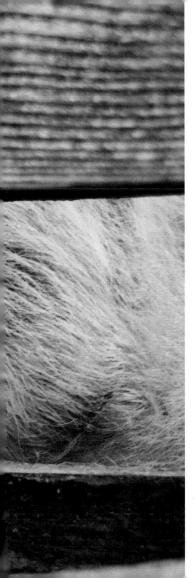

Even when I can't see you,
I know you're there for me.

No matter where our lives take us, know that we'll always have each other.

How blessed we are that
our paths have crossed.

Our friendship gives
me strength even
when I'm feeling weak.

You help me appreciate
the little things.

You are the big spoon
to my little spoon.

A great friend knows when you could use a great hug.

I can always be myself
when I'm with you.

It's not about the final destination, it's about the memories we made along the way.